An Audience of One

An Audience of One

POEMS BY
GERALD W. BARRAX

Athens
The University of Georgia Press

Copyright © 1980 by the University of Georgia Press
Athens 30602

All rights reserved

Set in 10 on 12 point Monticello type
Printed in the United States of America

Library of Congress Cataloging in Publication Data

Barrax, Gerald W
  An audience of one.

  (Contemporary poetry series)
  I. Title.
PS3552.A732A95   811'.5'4   79–3050
ISBN 0–8203–0500–6
ISBN 0–8203–0502–2 pbk.

"Near the End of a Savage Winter" © 1971
by the National Spiritual Assembly of the Bahá'ís
of the United States.

To the audience of one who made it possible.

Ic ǣnig ne mette wid de gelīc.

Acknowledgments

Acknowledgment is given to the following publications in which poems from this book first appeared.

Black World: "Visit," "Body Food"

Callaloo: "I Travel with Her," "Without Gaudy Flowers," "An Audience of One," "Last Letter," "Three Meetings"

Contemporary Poetry of North Carolina (1977): "Ghosts"

The Georgia Review: "He Goes around His World"

Hambone (Stanford University Committee for Black Performing Arts): "The Singer"

Journal of Black Poetry: "King: April 4, 1968," "Lovesong at Midsummer," "Fifth Dance Poem: To Violins in the Streets"

Nimrod: "Shani," "Narrative of a Surprising Conversion," "Ligustrum" (formerly titled "Barriers 6")

Obsidian: "There Were No Birds," "Hubris," "Confession," "Another Fellow," "Wings"

Poetry Northwest: "Big Bang"

Southern Poetry Review: "In the Restaurant," "There Was a Song," "Something I Know about Her," "Gift" (formerly titled "Barriers 1"), "Between Us and the World" (formerly titled "Barriers 2"), "The Passage of Shiva," "Moby Christ"

World Order: "Near the End of a Savage Winter"

Contents

IV · An Audience of One

I

An Exchange of Light

Last Letter

I might not have known his voice
And he would have known mine
As one-too-many wrong numbers
Except grief had deafened him
As your silence had terrified me of discoveries
As one day and another
And another had gone and no letter
No call came.

We were so good, so clever
We needed no third friend,
We had no one to tell me,
Who had no rights in your life.
He didn't say you were dead :
You were buried "just yesterday, just
Yesterday."
That deep trough in your back.
The small crease between your eyes.

In the Restaurant

I understand
Watching this public exposure
Of mere flesh that must be fed

Why I must keep away
From the tables of my enemies
Or lose them.

Poor creatures
Betrayed by this ritual
They don't know how vulnerable we are

When their heads go down
To meet their forks
It's a gesture too much like prayer

A cry for help, a plea for kinship.
Whether something else's predator or my own enemy
Dripping the blood of a warm kill

Between the jaws of either
Death holds us closer than hate
Feeding us mortality in such small portions.

Three Meetings

I: Atlanta

He has a room for her to belly dance in
but all he can see is her face,
her hands (he'll be able to swear to that);
nothing under her sensible suit
that he can see even winks, let alone
moves; the only dancing done
is 70 stories up around the Sun Dial,
an hour around the top of the city.
    Looking down there he thinks of DuBois
    standing on one of the Hundred Hills,
    his gigantic mind fusing the city with "swarthy Atalanta."
But addled by his conventional martinis
he remembers the wrong myth and the myth wrongly
and keeps wishing that just one golden apple
would fall for him;
below them, instead, the neon dome
of something out of blue—(from up here
the slow sun dance and her "funny drinks"
affecting their concern)—they can't tell what,
but decide on a blue mushroom.
No. A Blue Mushroom.
A thing different enough to make a difference:
it's what we expect from conventions anyway,
and the anonymity to tell more than we know.

At home he marvels that in spite of his temptation
to imagine her belly moving them that hour
around the sun, he touches her once all evening
just before parting, on the shoulder. She didn't
feel it, he's sure. Or drop a single apple.
It was that Blue Mushroom.

II: Vicksburg

He is forcing down a Spanish Omelet,
too sweet, and ignoring the dark brown bread
and whipped butter because
His stomach is in knots. He'd had to curse
and pray his car to start again
and get him here before she left.
He hadn't eaten. She sips
orange juice, perfectly
cool, the schoolteacher face above the collar
watching him. She never drinks
coffee in the summer. His omelet
is too hot and he sweats into his glasses.
His voice keeps going wrong.
They sit long past the breakfast hour
and the waitresses begin changing the tables for lunch.
They haven't talked long enough but he feels
they ought to go. Like the kind of lovers they are
they leave with no place to go
but to her car. It is hot. November
has given them, six days prematurely,
this July, for talk. She leaves
to go to the "ladies room." When she comes back
she takes off her jacket and his eyes dazzle
when he sees that her face
becomes throat and glowing shoulders, arms.
His mind goes crazy
thinking of brown cream, brown bread, brown
craziness. She turns into another woman.
There is a July light in the car
from her incredible shoulders,

6

glowing with the sweat that had been hidden
under the jacket.
His mind mumbles. His tongue forgets
and he says pretty when he means beautiful. She turns
on the seat and for the first time ever,
touches him,
both hands on both hands
and shines that light into his eyes.
His mind goes. His eyes go.
His tongue. They are all finished.
Almost nine months late
his hungers have brought him all these miles
for more food than his dazzled flesh can use
just to be touched and turned into another man.

III: New Orleans

1

In this city with its summer-leased apartment
they are again on neutral ground
and could be the first lovers in the world. Instead
they are having a seance in the park

materializing husbands and wives
out of the air and water of their zodiacs
they listen to their names
see them come out of their mouths
puffs of air

they have had to move from one expectant tree
to another to escape the sun down into

this cool dell
they sit on the earth against a tree
and like a boy he throws stones

when he kisses her shoulder the trees begin humming
in expectation and rigid happiness

but they are content to talk ghosts into sunlight
and nothing more

the trees wait and wait
feeling nothing from the earth
but the vibration of voices
    with the memory of the quick heartbeat of squirrels
and honest hot sparrows and jays in their leaves

the trees begin throwing stones

they are ashamed that they are not naked
and have neither life nor knowledge

They are ghosts of water and air
and conjure up others instead of blessing
the hot trees

the trees are throwing stones

Driven away
they come to a bridge that has wept for them
the kind of lovers they are
they discover they cannot cross
running water

walking back and forth
on the bridge she is smiling at the ghost
behind the god
awful camera.

2

He has gone and she is preparing to leave
Him to haunt the apartment from that brief visit.
She sees the chair where he sat at the table typing.
There the sofa he sat, eating lettuce and tomato
Sandwich and beer.
Here the arch between the rooms where
They stood arms around, ten seconds,
Too soon to ever relive the feel.

Outside on the landing
Butterflies flew into their mouths
To say goodbye.

3

Meanwhile
Now that he is safely home
She writes him from the apartment
"Was there anything that you
forgot to tell me, ask me, or do?"
And he is sitting confounded
In single seance at a round white table,
Staring into the trees ranged
Across his back yard.
His mind gone the vision comes

9

he sees now what would have been his own
back, kneeling
at the sofa her legs
around him they are half naked
wearing the red polka dot and
dark brown Ban-Lon his ass rotating it
into her she smiles at him over his own
shoulder into the god
awful
Eyes of the unborn ghost
Sitting at his lawn table,
Waiting for the rigid indignant Maple
Dogwood, Oak, Willow Willow, Pine
And Crab Apple to destroy his fences. Right now
He hears them laughing. The toodstools are growing
And already the brown grass is filling up with stones.

There Were No Birds

There were no birds anywhere
Until I realized how the mask was kept in place:
You sat in my chair, eyes on me, always
Listening—your silences creating vacuums
In which my constant babble betrayed me—
And I remembered your hands with the long long fingers
Making their own fragile cage in your lap,
Whose stillness was as impressive as yours;
  Until I remembered the two of us turning
In our car seats after my last goodbye kiss too many
And those slender brown birds suddenly breaking
Away and flying for me, winging around my shoulder and
  drawing me into your stillness and
Finding their mute tongues in our mouths at last.

King: April 4, 1968
For Eva Ray

When I was a child
in the Fall the axes fell
in Alabama and I tried
to be somewhere else,
but the squeals of the pigs dying
and hogs and the sight of their
opened throats were everywhere.

I wasn't given that kind of stomach.

When I was 14 I killed
the last thing bigger than a mouse
with my Daisy Red Ryder:
a fat robin on a telephone wire,
still singing,
as my first shot went high
I sighted down and HEARD from where I was
the soft thud of the copper pellet in his
fat red breast. It just stopped
and fell over backwards
and I had run away
before it hit the ground, taking
my stomach with me.

I'll never know about people—
if the soft thing in the gut can be cut out—
because I missed all the wars—
but when I learned that non
violence kills you anyway
I wished

12

I wished I could do it I wished I
could
do you know what it means to wish
you could kill, to
wish you were given that?

But I am
me. Whatever made me made
you, and I anesthetize the soft thing
to stop squirming when
you do it brothers I shout
righton, righton, rightON
my heart is with you
though my stomach is still in Alabama pig
pens.

The Singer
For Nina, Roberta, Aretha.
Sarah, Ella, Carmen.
Dinah, Billie, Bessie. And Ma.

Black Angel
Doing what she's gotta do
The sister sings

"Like a stone bird"
He said, intending to praise her.
But no bird has such a choice.

They speak, too,
Or whatever twittering means
But does that explain human song?

Maybe this more than natural impulse
Surprised even the creator
Who let the possibility

Slip his mind.
Not unintended.
Just not thought of.

　　Suppose
There was a creature
not yet human
who cocked his head, dimly quizzical
at birdsong
and did something—
roared, screeched, howled—
something purely joyous in imitation
and those birds filled the prehistoric air
in flight from his obscenity.

14

Who was to tell him
he wasn't created for that? Or
        suppose Eve.
Giving a name
to something dull Adam
didn't know about:

   What's that? What are you doing?

And she, holding the doomed child,
stopped and looked at him as if listening
and smiled, and said

   Singing.

Not like birds
Who are doomed to sing
Her doom and ours is her silence.
        The sisters sing
        Doing what they've gotta do
        Black Angels.

Without Gaudy Flowers

From such a distance as ours
we couldn't begin
like lovers who have only their bodies.
Who live in them
and become what they have and expect to get
from tryst to tryst.
Who save for one another, themselves,
the orgasmic releases from perfect
tensions beteween hard organs and soft;
sometimes hiding in their bodies from wives and husbands
whose claims may leave them nothing.
Who may not be without love but whose identities
are what they can deliver.

From our distance, little details
began sprouting from letters like hesitant tendrils,
groping toward each other in names, dates, trivia;
simple truths; secrets. Green confessions
fingering down through the small ground we claimed.
And rooting there.
At intervals we met and became what our bodies demanded.
Between, we greened ourselves:
in short visits to public places (like phanerogams
we stole, from whoever noticed us, approval for the love
that flowered in the visible marriage of hands and eyes),
in parks, woods (like orphans, where hungry trees
adopted us
and used our memories to become conscious
of one another);
in letters where each detail added a feature or gesture

16

to our own identities:
    when finally you wrote about someone
    of whose existence I hadn't known, you told me
    "She is the kind of friend you would be
    if you were a woman"
then I felt the quick surprise of our lovers' bodies
confused between desire and its transcendence
as buds unfolded from our nipples,
feathery willow began its slow growth
over your head and genitals,
and I was covered with peperomia,
in the crisp leaves of emerald ripple.

Now driving through these smoky mountains
back toward you
I see you giving contours to the blue hills
that lie on all my horizons;
each green cell signals
from your body to mine
that they have claimed us
for purposes greater than our own.

I look across the valleys
and am astonished to discover
even without the gaudy flowers
how well we have survived the seasons.

An Exchange of Light

Her husband away again, she busies herself
Moving her green amorous children from room
To room to find the sun in the house so tastefully
Decorated with her own ceramics, textured
Walls, draperies, and other products of all
Those classes. "They are my babies," she says, touching
The leaf of the ficus (but smiling at her son, too;
She will have no more). "Several of them have histories
Of illness, survival stories.
The begonia (that's my red Chinese ginger jar)
Was unwatered during my last convention
Trip. You see the spot bare of leaves. They all
Missed my care, my music." She touches a fantastic
Dieffenbachia. "Would you believe I have
an orgasmic response to their beauty?
In winter I burn gro-lights because the house
Is always too dark for the number of them that need the sun."

(But I have a picture of you sitting
Among split-leaf philodendrons moved from the fence
In their pots to surround you in an exchange of light.
You smile at the absurdity of him and me,
One behind the one behind the camera.
I see you jogging on the beach.
Your hands were full of the shells you brought me,
Hands as fragile as the gift. Under you
My hands became diviners and I found the sea
Filling the long trough of your back. We had
Eaten the golden apples and the juice was in your mouth,
The seeds in mine. Under you my limbs and

Roots grew up towards air and water,
Meeting the tendrils you sent down
To crack through skull and heart to our seedbed,
Our own leaves surrounding us, my palms covering
Your breasts, you holding my face above the water,
You take the seeds back from my mouth the moment
Just before I drown. I have this picture.
Does anyone there know that someone needed you like that?)

Visit

She holds to the idea
of a husband and three sons.
The accomplishment of it.
My three years away
she holds as hostages
and we move and place each other in cities
whose names become the bonds that hold us.
　　Eventually I must travel from Durham to Clarksburg,
　　　　the days on Eldora Place
　　　　　like the memory of childhood, or water,
　　　　　　the house and park deceiving us with permanence
　　　　　　into playing house with real kids.

After eight months
I am saddened that sons can grow so tall
in the absence of their father.

　　　　*

Sunday evening we fished in Buffalo Lake
and I discovered that a father must not think of the worm
when baiting a hook for a son,
and little Blue Gills must be killed outright
if they swallow it.
Cold blooded things,
what must a daddy do
when his youngest son brings a fish
hooked through the head and one eye
but pull it out.
It's a sport
and I believe it's said
they feel no pain.
They bleed, but feel no pain.

20

II

A Means of Travel

A Means of Travel

I got to 17 with all my parts
when tonsils were cheap enough
for parents to excuse themselves for sickly sons.
So mine came out.
As long as I was there
I decided to give up that piece of flesh
I was more familiar with.
    (a footnote here
    would expose my precocious ignorance
    in my envy of the skinless boys in the school pool,
    once believing they knew something
    useless for me to lie about—
    believing that foreskins somehow disappeared into
    or were snatched away by
    whatever girls had that I hadn't.
    But by 17 I'd had my books
    in plain brown wrappers under the mattress
    and knew better,
    but not much)

Home from the hospital
and just about to graduate,
the girl with whom I'd practiced
kissing to death
gave me a poem.
It was for my throat
(she knowing only half of what I'd lost).
    I was impressed.
And being too sore anyway
in more places than one

to even ask for more.
I wrote one back to her.

Ellen,
whatever has become of you,
I thank you for teaching me
to sublimate the discomfort of my throat
and the agony of my stitched and bandaged dick
into a means of travel.

There Was a Song

There was a song
she pulled out of the trees
as she walked her way
toes pointed slightly inward,
whistling like a young boy.

There was that song
she held in her hands
that might have been the sea.
She was afraid of that,
but in her hands
it became a song, simply,
or the sound of something
without leaves or feathers.

There was she
with something of the trees
and the sea in her hands after all
and that walk that took her about the island.
  And although nobody called
  I heard her;
  although nobody called
  I followed.

The Only Way My Dumb Flesh Knows

With no faith in the memory of my cells
I enslave myself to a box
where the light shines through the clicking eye
and fixes my soul in those 60 seconds
before the buzzer stops or the beep calls me.
I keep looking back to you all for this,
the only way my dumb flesh knows.
You never move.
You keep:in the same naked spaces
in my mind
the special places I have where I hide to find you.

You keep,reading your book to ignore me
    as I make a tripod of elbow and knees click

You keep walking toward me naked frozen stride
    distorting the pale triangle lengthening curves
    that boomeranged my ego to silence.
    Losing my head once I took yours off your picture,
    sacrificing the consolation of your . eyes.
    But the articulate knees. The belly's eye. The dark areolas
    clickclick

And oh you keep your ankles crossed over your head
    smiling through your knees on my bed, the most wickedly
    posed sitting on the back of my green
    chair, your feet on the arms
    looking down at the up shot clicklick

And you,have remained out of focus
    my frenzy for detail getting me too close
    blurring my truer eye
    in trying to see myself in yours
    and in there, and there cliclic

And for you the last I perfected techniques
    and keep you more than any
    getting myself timed and distanced in place with you
    to picture that lovely beast with two backs
    or reversed, the androgynous anthropophagi
    creature from another country
    where lovers grow loving heads between their legs clilic

And no matter when I look
I can never surprise any of your eyes
not being kind.
They never change.
You know:I never will forget you for that
and you, or you, and you
because I have you clicked to keep.

Lovesong at Midsummer

Long before she left
I had become a Tantalus
Reaching for the small pendants
She swung above my head.
I could taste the way she flowed from my thirst.
Taller than she,
When I spoke through the random media
In which I waited
It was above her eyes, lowered away from me
Whenever she expected me to say
Love.
When I said "love" at all for us
I felt as much horror in the pauses
Where words were crushed to flecks of silence
Between the teeth of her kindness
As in the sound of hurrying chariots.
I had at least a half demented summer of her.

Then she filled her pockets with crocus and bluebells
Her breasts with hummingbirds
Caught butterflies in her hair

And spilling sunlight
through her brown fingers
She went
         tearing the guts out of summer.

Fifth Dance Poem: To Violins in the Streets

See our first A B C's
hear them in the air like gangbusters
sounds like death,
lead pipes and gunbutts crunching skulls,
gargling and screaming in our masters' voices,
Mad Dog Coll making crime pay for cereals and bath soaps.
See
    men dying in the little garish windows
of comic/funny books
where lovingly muscled
capewearing leotarded superWhite
heroes
choreographed for heroic poses
demolish evil scientists
who only want to rule
the world of White Heroes.

See
    the Saturday afternoon lessons
death riding easy across the prairie
move the wagons   ring around your destiny
Men Who Feast on Destiny
feast of the red man's buffalo flesh
    This week:
                note the impact of .45 slugs
                fired from the Peacemakers
                of whitehatted whitehorsed whiteskinned
heroes

See
    the bonanza of sound

moving again as picture primer
to the G.I.'s in the Good War.
See how to twistpull a bayonet out of a gut.
See how to hold the hand over the mouth and slit a throat.
See how to win the world for demockery again
with those son
of a gun-
ning gosh
durning trueblue intrepid soldierboyWhite
heroes.
There were no others
it seems.

See

  the post-graduate, T V's blessings,
the culture time capsule pre-
serving it all

And new things too

The Real Thing
there in the livingroom
the obscenity for our children to see
the destroyer of a White
Hero
getting the reallive primetime gutshot.
Ph.D.

Now see
my Brothers the bread losers

do it to Property
or, irritated by the murder of a Black Hero
by a white
one
do it to where they live
do it to Property.

Those viOlent
        Othose
viOlent tsk niggers tsktsk.

I Travel with Her

1. How we look

Traveling with her
between marriages I found
was a way of picturing things lost
back into my life.
I do it each year on the exact dates, or between,
by slipping into photos
that show where we've been.

    In disguise the first year,
apprehensive about names and hotel registers
in Paris and London we appear
together only three times,
not even chancing
passing friendly natives:
      once using the timer I got us lying across the bed
in the Hotel du Mont Blanc studying the map
for the next day's pictures;
      and twice at Stratford
because we met Jan,
someone from home who knew too little about the Polaroid
to be afraid to use mine.
Otherwise, the two of us look out at me—
the camera, each, separate, alone.

2. What we saw

All the expected sights are there
(count them:name them one by one)
but I felt uneasy about what I didn't get.

32

On our second morning in Paris
she was awakened at seven
by a girl singing *Santa Lucia* in the street below
accompanied by someone on a violin.
She supposed they were from the Sorbonne
just down the street.
Imagine that happening anywhere back home,
we mused, when I awoke.

A year later she was home in the Caribbean,
ten years gone, with me along.
This time we both heard the flute,
terrifying her,
at first looking and mistakenly recognizing Brown,
the ghost of her youth
who had smelled or heard Death
from whatever island he hobbled on his goat foot
to hang back at the ends of funeral processions.
He had always played, she said, *Abide With Me*.
Shades of Black Pan, then and now.
But not Brown this Sunday. This time a blind one
with a boy outside,
the flute weird wailing
hymns for alms.
    I didn't look out,
    I have no pictures of it,
    so as in Paris I don't know for myself.

    But I know
the danger of being too often behind the lens,

too often not having proof of myself;
I know the possibilities of traveling
in the wrong direction
in the opposite way
and with my camera empty
maybe never getting back.

She Listens to Madrigals

Take, O take those lips away
That so sweetly were forsworn

Old sweat, the sun, perfume.

The lances dip toward her.
She favors one
But she knows her Freud
As well as any
And closes her legs
Tighter.

The lute plays on her dreaming.

She is assaulted by color,
Livery and armor
Sunstruck in cinerama.
The pennants flutter. She hears
The flourish of long trumpets
Behind the intricate voices.
Fa la la.

. . . those eyes, the break of day,
Lights that do mislead the morn

The sun. Hooves tear up the green turf.
She itches and crawls beneath the colors.
She has not bathed either
To make it as real as she knows it was.

The lutes play on her dreaming.

The lances gallop toward each other
And her favor ripples from the tip of the Black Knight's.
She closes her legs tighter.

But my kisses bring again, bring again,
Seals of love, but sealed in vain, sealed in vain

Her perfect lover, perfect in love, perfect in time
Bows over her hand.
His hair crawls. She holds her breath.
    Smile.
She knows the code demands no more
But is assaulted by hope

As the lances splinter on her symbols of the sun:
The white, the black. The dead wood flowers
Into roses. Her legs
Open and she has returned.
Take, O take those lips away.

The Fourth Son

Halfway through my life I've lived one quarter
of it to create the persistence of memory
in the memory of the rest. More and
more I lose my place, being lulled

Offguard as a sleepy reader: I blink
and discover between period and
capital that some part of my life has
flashed and gone—or that I've been somewhere and back.

I'm always most unprepared for my sons.
They flicker in and out in the random
stages of growth arrested for the rest
of my life by the six years between us

    today. I carry four-year-old Josh
    in one arm to preschool because it was
    so cold and I want to get them there fast;
    fathers sometimes need excuses to hold
    the warmth they love, I never did; Jerry
    I pull along with the other hand, such
    long legs to be only six, was Dennis
    on school patrol? yes Dennis the missing
    son has left early for school patrol. When

I'm back on the page *this time I know*
why you've come: today: my new wife

was told that the child we carried
to the hospital two weeks ago

37

in the plastic bowl proved under the
microscope to have been a perfect

boy, naturally. This time then you'd
come for the son that would've been half your
brother. We hadn't told you. When you visit
next summer, I don't know if we will.

Something I Know about Her

She touches when she talks—
must touch to smooth out syntax with her fingertips,
must lay on her hand to hear her echo,
to feel the words you don't speak
below the ones you do.

What she means by it is warm;
if she touches you, listen:
to surprise her at it
    would be like waking a sleepwalker
    between two dreams—
would trap her in this tedious
world of mere jive words.

Shani

1

Your miraculous conception
was too improbable to be doubted,
to be anything but a human
success: to the very day
following the seven lean years,
to the very April that second-named you
when your mother and I,
naked in the innocence of others' lives,
walked a dying afternoon through a greenhouse.
Whatever there was among those exotic flowers
that yessed us got into her
and drove her
    life and will
towards you, seven Decembers away.

2

We had expected you
the year before.
A boy came. We grieved for him,
losing the struggle to out-
grow the benign tumors,
the weeds choking him
out, a flayed plum.
The womb made whole again
they took you, without labor,
on the afternoon your mother timed
to end the next year.
    Three generations of sons

had kept watch for you,
but waiting with the stubbornness of your sign,
you took your own and the world's
good time to be born a woman.

3

Halfway through your blind swim
toward us, deeper than need for reason
you made for my hand at that living wall,
touched it once,
and the half-playful certainty I gave your mother
became real for me.
We chose the name, then, for her,
whose need for you exceeded denial,
but whose belief had resigned her to sons:
Shani: the wonder, the surprise, the start-
ling event.

4

From under the ocean
where the slave ships once drove
between cold England and St. Vincent
your mother's parents bequeathed you
the sea changes of your Caribbean heritage.
On her side,
on that green Gem of the Antilles

that glows on your wall,
daughters are no less rare
for not being so.

All through the North
your paternal kin remained exiled
in winter and cities,
still the alien places
long after the Great Migration
from the black soil of our origins.
They waited for word of you.
It had to be here, Home
where December goes out green,
in this South where the last daughter was born.

You arrived as you did,
the year ended, the next began
as if none of you intended
to ever hear of winter again.

5

When I was told they almost severed
the cord that bled you both
I thought of the boy who wouldn't have been you—
    whose pain ended last year
        that wouldn't be yours—
and of my three living sons in that first life before death
lost in the ruins of a marriage

and whose loss is you
and will always be yours.

The burden of each day's guilt
is to deny or balance
the claims of our confusions.
Between the green winters of this second life
and the fatherless profit and loss of the last,
which is the weight,
which the counterweight?

The distant brothers
come for 30 days a year
to make us whole again.

III

Ghosts

Ghosts

Young and talented, they were so good
With words they had lines to throw away
Or they sang and he made any stringed instrument
Do clever things behind, under, or around
Her voice. Their best
Was a thing on death that made it
A kind of fool: they loved each other
So much.
              When he started losing her
It was one room at a time
After she'd been the first to learn
She'd watched and felt the rooms changing
Watched her knees unflex
And when her thighs sank below her own horizon
And she saw what he was doing
There the look turned both their bodies to stone and salt.
              To be able to let her go
He had to follow her back
Through all the rooms she'd been dying in
And dream she was dead. He dreamed it.
He wrote and sang songs for himself
That would've moved stones or
Death itself if she had been dead.
Then she let him let her go, resurrected
From that house because in everything
They had said whether very clever or merely true
Each would've given back the other's life
To become a stranger in someone else's.
              At first he marveled to be still alive until

He walked from room to room in that house
Afraid to ever look back
And learned that death is less than half of dying.

The Evolution

She used to sit, childless
among the creatures he had named
who brought their young
to hear her approving laughter.
She had guessed the secret of their origin
lay in that nameless act
in which she saw the females, stiff-legged
quake under the rearing
and savage thrusting of their mates,
their cries so different from her own
when she and the man met in sheer surprise.
Yet they, not she, bore young
and when her thighs held nuzzling cubs
against her belly
and she felt the ache inside
she wondered if immortality was reward enough.
And her thighs could contain him, too, with ease
but not themselves
    (he roamed between them
    wondering what her need could mean.
    Long afterwards he remembered
    and yearned, seeing her pain,
    to know the moment when
    he had engendered Cain).

He Goes around His World

Lately he's begun to wonder
about different ways
to get his body where he's going.
He got to where he is mostly
untraveled, unexplored himself by anyone
except for two so like himself
but that they knew so surely
what women they were.

Now, although no contortionist,
he has to go around his own world
to see his sights.

No longer young
he's learned to bend his bones
before they break.

No electrician
he's learned to connect
and close all his circuits.

Still younger than ever
he's willing to try anything
once to get him anywhere.

Two Poems

1

I can spare you this sunlight (open
carefully) because once
when my trees were bare
your letter made them rain outside
my window, inside, and made a difference
on a day when I could see none
anywhere.

2

That funny sound is
the two of us loving you:
your three hearts beating.

Narrative of a Surprising Conversion

Guidance counselors at the liberal
integrated northern high school
told the boy after taking written
aptitude tests
that they showed
how good he was with his hands.
That something like carpentry
or auto mechanics
was what he was for.
    He was amazed.
    How could they tell?
    How could they know? He decided then that
white folks must know everything. He'd
wanted to be a pharmacist a lawyer an
engineer or a writer a doctor ETC but
none of these
needed the kind of manual dexterity he
never knew he
had, and since they knew
better, he knew in his
awe it was no use. Instead then of
worrying about college any more
and medicine engineering writing ETC he used his hands to
deal, to steal, ETC, i.e., to survive. And when the time
came, instead of being
uselessly out of the way in an
office a classroom on a
bridge ETC when the time came
he was there—
when it was spring or summer on green maps

and somewhere melons were bursting red meat into the sun,
on his block it was the uncertain season
between the cold trickle of black rivulets into gutters
and the slap of the sun's red palm on concrete—
then his long supple black hands curved around the rifle
and the finger lifted from his life
and curved around and oh gently squeezed
and the top of a silky head novaed into the red sun.
And then it knew everything.

Sixth Dance Poem

We survived the pyre of the bed
On the evening of the longest day we ever knew
Midwifing each other we rose
Bloody newborns
You as twin to me as pulse and heart

Then I know I saw
you dancing light back
into the room before
the bed the altar where I
sat watching who may
have been myself—costume,
taped music, chor-
eography all yours
but with no breath no
blood in you that was not my own

I know I saw you danc-
ing your subtle hands un-
able to distract my eyes
from the ecliptic your belly and hips
made through the solstices
the equinoxes of our sidereal room

I know I saw you dancing
Yet when there's need to make lovework again
The woman in our bed is not the woman love set dancing
    (the disco moves together
    autonomous but one)
And I begin to hear the shadow of a second heart,
Another breathing:

"Hard work" I say "Yes it is for you" she says watching me
Choreograph all our moves
   (the ballroom style leading
   and following)
Watching my erratic solo orbit around her still center
Its apogee sending me out alone
Out where gravity
Lets go
At the limits of her attraction

Where did you go
The one whose body once
Did that dancing?

Body Food

Oh my Brothers
you who need it
it is your right
to turn to what
you believe is the true
God or any other
but what do you think
kept your great & grand
papas & mamas alive long
& strong enough to give you
the strength to make the choice?:
to take a faith with roots
which their spirits yearned back for
while their blood hallowed
the cradles out of which your flesh
came into this wilderness?
    You their children
know better than the masters
who were ignorant of the strength it took
to begin with to survive;
what little they had was given grudgingly
without the suspicion of what
those strong men & strong
women could make of leavings.
    If then it is in the blood of some of us
to lust after the ears the tails the snouts
the feet the maws & even the
chitlins of the filthy beast
forgive us: with these
& the greens cornbread & molasses

that transubstantiated into the bones
brain & flesh of the black household gods
who brought us through the evil
rooted in this land,
    we honor them
in the heritage of their strength.

An Old Man Feels His Age in the Adult Book Store

The eye is still a camera.
This slick paper has edges
That slice deeper than laughter
At the tears of old men
For what the big boys do;
Makes wounds wider than fear
Touching the timids' minds' edges.
Slick paper with edges that slice deeper
Than any woman's refusal.

Still the eye is a camera
Oh lady for pity even
Oh god girl
would do you no wrong
And there's no relief in growing older.
Each year the closeups become closer up
In colors more living than mine.
My wishes overflow my hands
And the hooded eyes that wink below their bellies
Capture our absurd poses
That cry for sympathy and belief.

"I had a terror—since September"

First a terror of choice, but that was done
By September—Renunciation my chosen word.
I hope she knows the troubles, what pools I wade,
What an old romantic ass I've become—
To remember each stage of that delirium
I bought the albums and use the music we heard
To keep us in time together out of handmade
Memories of loving and scrooving in double-tongue.
Double-stopped now, it's all I can do to hum
The tunes and hang on to what I can, less
Each September, channeling raw music into the wound—
Afraid when she appears in the room
As out of time as music from all this sound
I might say yes this time goddamn I'd say yes.

Hubris

As if powered by her bumper stickers,
"I Found It" on one side
and on the right, "This is a God
                    Squad Car,"
CB antenna on top and going
like an angel out of hell, she left behind
this sinner driving Oh so carefully
with his buckled-in daughter
in the 25 mph zone.

Confession

They tapped your spine
When you were two
And the microscope showed bacteria in
the fluid—a surprise: your
Symptoms suggested only
A virus. But they'd keep you
To see if a culture grew, just
To be sure. Your mother swayed.
She never left you the next four days
While you lay with the tube they'd looked
Everywhere to find a vein for.

That first night she prayed for
The miracle. At home
I called your grandmother
Up North. She too said she'd pray
For you and told me to
Do the same. I said yes
And stayed awake a long
Time deciding not to and
Reading. I hadn't before.
How could I begin with something
So important as an only daughter?
Shani, two prayers and maybe more
Went out or
Up, but not mine in a night
Whose horror was equal to its
Chance of being you and not
Some other whose recovery might not be better than death.
A martini puts me to sleep when nothing will.

The next day there was a miracle. But the next day
Our mothers
Were no longer believing in or needing
Miracles: they knew
What it was. I said nothing.
But when you came home
Free of the tube and bottle
I first knew the danger of ruining you
For life. All it takes
Is to remember you there
And no matter what you do
It will never be the same
Because God one night
Happened to have been a
Lab Technician who left a careless
Thumbprint on a glass slide.

IV

An Audience of One

Gift

What does it mean
that there is a snake lying among the wild strawberries;
   Spring has laid smooth stones
     at the edge of the pool;
  there are birds who see farther at night
    than the warm things under cover of purple leaves?
Some god has bitten this mottled apple.
We swim in these summer days, its juices.
What does it matter where the snake hides:
   I was out of place until a blue jay
   in return for my seed
   left that black banded feather from his wing
   in my back yard.

Between Us and the World

The heart relaxes one beat
and dark rain cools the rough skin,
breathing eases,
lungs, needles, and leaves
go out and into the air, ex-
changing molecules between us and the world,
the power in that one light
moves live substances through our systems
like creatures beneath surface tension,
corpuscles oxygenating the sap,
the tingling of photocells
synthesizing sunlight in the blood
to feed the root systems out of the heart
and send the love in the bowels
up the shaft of that power
to these leaves flaming their tips
out into air again.
In the systole
My blood is driven from the chambers of the heart
And extinguishes the fire. My breath withers
The leaves. My mind blasts the roots
From the earth; and the trees howl at the return
Of consciousness and the darkness that was, before
The rain.

Another Fellow

The almost whole skin
Lay right outside the window of my basement
Where I'd been entombed for more than a year.
Whenever it happened, if I had raised myself
And looked out of the groundlevel window
I'd have seen it crawling out of its year-old skin;
It would've seen a face marveling and envious
Up from a book behind the screen,
But it would've been too busy
Doing what it was supposed to do
To stop for me;
My ancestors, considering its immortality,
Would've welcomed it with food and drink
When it came as spirit of the living-dead from the forest
To visit their huts;
And I would've sacrificed a book to its wisdom
In return for a poem.
    Dear Emily,
That was in September, months ago.
The grass after days of rain was high, wet, still growing
And had to be cut once more for the year. I cut it
In anticipation, wondering if I would drive it
Into the square of the yard, or out,
Half dreading both but needing
One or the other. This year I will be 43.
I found neither the spotted shaft in the high grass
Nor in my room your worm transformed
And ringed with power. I found an empty skin
That I threw over the fence.

Wings

It can look like a summons when things
Come at you like that:
Even for birds I love
Its appearance was too sudden,
And I still didn't know whose terror
I felt, looking up
Into the summer peace
At the flurry of gray wings
Breaking up the sun at my window.

Big Bang

Some kind of flying insect—
its existence beginning
only in my periphery
and ending at the windshield,
                                    exploding
in death, the yellow shape
a galaxy.

Between those worlds and me
just right of eye level
other systems are coming into being
worlds without end.

If I can push a button and bring water,
turn a knob and wipe it all away,
why not someone else?

The Passage of Shiva

Usually I make better time at night
but starting out at 3 a.m.
there's no place as dark as North Carolina
driving 501 miles north to West Virginia
black as the inside of a (   )
it's their element,
things crossing the road
unnerving me to slow down:
the prey and predators not knowing that the roads say
the world is no longer theirs.

Even cats, who know us so well
        we hate them for their stealth,
when they come to our roads cross them
as blindly as they were built

and I discovered about myself
that I have as much dread of running down
one of those hotly pursuing or pursued
as a man.
                        And I did.
Leaping into the lights
somebody's dog after nobody's rabbit
hit in midstride, one bite away.

What apocalypse did I bring?
Surely for the prey it was a visitation—
a nova of deliverance:
some passing god or Urban historian
who saw and rendered immediate justice at 60 mph.

70

For the dog, the death of a hunter,
the Great Hunter's terrible swift wheels
sending him to eternal good hunting
where the scent was "for ever warm
and still to be enjoyed."

A rationalization, perhaps,
but the road was mine anyway. Ours.

Coming back
I drove all day
when the burrows are carpeted with fur
and cats lie under cool porches
dreaming of cool and bountiful nights.

Ligustrum

A red spider, delicate, is traveling from the sun
Down the shadows of the Ligustrum.
One branch stirs against the screen,
Nudging October through my window.
    "Hardy hedge plant of the olive family.
    cultivated as an ornamental."
Red spider, travel down into the shadows.
Play, children. Bark,dogs. October
Day,sing.
    "Some varieties have persistent
    semi-evergreen foliage" . . .

. . . it does feel that way—
Those delicate feet skating
My waxy surface:
And that wasn't just the *wind* pushing my screen . . .

It is more than the wind, or October—that presence
Nodding welcome in the next leaf . . .
    "The oval or oblong leaves are about
    one to one and one half inches long."
No: it's the whole bush and the wind
Going through. "In early summer" we had white flower
Clusters, then the black berries.
    Kids, birds, spider: I have all these nerves
    now to feel you walking delicate feet
    and shouting October through the leaves,
    more ears than the wind.
"Native to northern China. Amur Privet, also called
Amur River Privet."

The spider on its way down the bush
from time to time goes to the tip of a leaf
and waves half its body and legs out into the sun.
We don't know why it does that.

Black Cat

We saw it sliding into the earth
through an open sewer—
slinking, she called it
with her ordinary distaste for cats.
But it slid down,
the tip of a black tongue
sucked back through iron lips.

I was there two days later
two blocks away, when something
poked the tongue back into light
through the asphalt mask
pressed upon the earth.
It half emerged and saw me
and we looked at each other
for as long as it commanded—
I frozen with one hand
on the cardoor handle,
it resting half in
half out of the earth,
more than half sphinx
less than half mortal.
It was early morning
and I had been tricked into belief
in eternal sunrise,
but the creature must have been there
        before this sun
when all eyes were yellow-green
less for looking away from light
than into darkness—

when only such eyes were needed
to distinguish beast from man,
the hunter from the killer.

Something flickered back into the green-yellow eyes
and dismissed me back into my sun
to my own destruction
beyond the need of hunting
through the long passages under the foundations
we live on.

Moby Christ

Again, Father,
I've tried to escape the tyranny of your right hand—
how many times among those fools who never know me
until it's too late
and now as lord of these hosts of the waters.

Again, Father,
you've searched me out—
once Judas
and now the divine madness of an old man
to hound me down to the sea like an animal.

My scars multiply:
you'll fill my skin with harpoons
as you've filled my memory with your crosses—
what I must pay
to put spirit into flesh,
to feel, God, to feel
even the pain.
You are old, Father,
a fond and foolish old man
who has never known that much
about what you've created.

    My hosts will pay, too.
Men believe I once died for their sins
and now these great creatures will die for mine:
    there go the ships, Father,
on your wide sea which your wanton boys
will wash in Leviathan's blood
and hunt down to extinction.

76

When the sea gives up its dead
Father
will nothing rise from its depths
but the fools who have crawled over the earth?

Near the End of a Savage Winter

In the beginning
winter came disguised in hesitation
and hung back from the blaze of autumn
into the mild year's end
when we celebrated an arbitrary birthday
still needing something not there
and impatient children
went sledding down the pure white hills
imagined on livingroom carpets.

Their redemption came with the first snow
and ours
when the temperature dropped
and the cold
separated us from memory,
probing white fingers
into our bellies and minds
and finding them full
and suitably lulled
by the ways of the world.

Now in the midst of our hungers
we wait in perfect faith
for spring   believing
its coming is inevitable
every year, every year. Every year.

But what lies under the snow
proves that what we have done
is not to be done

for each year the wounds deepen
the channels thicken with waste
and healing becomes more difficult.

We could not survive such cold.

The one eye of the sun.
The one eye of the moon.
The one eye of winter
: these malignant Cyclops have watched us
make the easy acceptances between lion and lamb
too long.
We wait for March and transition
salvation in the lamb
but we can not survive the cold
    and ice hangs under the rocky hillsides
    as opaque as frozen salt
    smooth as bands of muscle in a giant's thigh
and curbed by the sidewalks
lies uncoiled in black humps along the gutters.

The Buffalo Ghosts

In the black windows
The buffalo ghosts are eating the sweet grass
Growing in all the alleys
And main streets of the world.

An Audience of One

It's all very friendly
the way the night is shrieking
a joyful noise unto itself.

My area light is a baton
against the green that's too brilliant
and the absolute-black interstices of the wall of trees,
all in their perfect places: willows on the left,
oak to the right, maple, pine, and dogwood
orchestrated between, all leaning hungrily toward it,
swallowing the light
that goes into the woods and never
out again.
In there the hunger rages,
so close to my domicile,
things in combat to devour
one another, not at all
the way lovers do.

As an audience of one
it must be me to cough
and applaud the crickets, tree
frogs, and God knows what else
out there.
And I'm discovered.
Monitored,
I'm a terminal whose readouts are taken
and my internal processes fed back into the dark
where it is computed that you are gone from me,
in another part of that world.

81

Nothing stops completely,
not even the sanest music;
but in sympathy that great heartbeat slows down
and there is a diminuendo in the dark
while the trees and I lean toward
that cool artificial light
as though it were you or the sun.

Other Titles in the Contemporary Poetry Series